The Legend of the North Star

by Emily Bluestone
Illustrated by Vicki Bradley

Glenview, Illinois • Boston, Massachusetts • Chandler, Arizona
Upper Saddle River, New Jersey

stars

How did the North Star get into the sky? The Paiute (pi YOOT) Indians imagined this story.

The sky overhead is filled with stars at night. Have you noticed that these stars seem to move?

The Paiute Indians believe that people they called the People of the Sky moved through the sky at night. The People of the Sky made trails in the sky as they moved. The Paiute Indians believe that stars used these trails to move through the sky. That is why almost every star except one is in a different place each night.

Paiute: Native American tribe living in parts of California, Nevada, Utah, Arizona, and Oregon

mountain

    Only the North Star stays in the same place night after night. This is its story.
    A long, long time ago, a mountain sheep called Na-gah lived on Earth. He lived with his father. Na-gah's father's name was Shinoh. Na-gah and Shinoh were People of the Sky.
    Na-gah was the strongest and bravest of all the mountain sheep. He could climb the tallest mountains. Shinoh was very proud of his son.
    One day, Na-gah traveled very, very far. He saw a tall, rocky mountain. He was sure he could climb it!

Na-gah walked around the mountain many times. But he could not find a way to get to the top.

I must find a way up. I must find a trail or a path that goes to the top of the mountain, he thought. *My father will be so proud of me if I can climb to the top.*

At last, Na-gah found a crack in a rock. He squeezed through the crack and went inside the mountain. It was very dark inside the mountain. Na-gah could not see anything.

Then Na-gah found a path that went up and up. Na-gah thought this path might be the path to the top of the mountain.

mountain sheep

Na-gah walked up the path. It was full of rocks. He stepped carefully, but some of the rocks crashed to the bottom.

Maybe I should go back, Na-gah thought. But when he looked behind him, he saw that the falling rocks had blocked the path. Na-gah had no choice. He had to keep climbing.

Na-gah climbed and climbed. His body began to hurt. Na-gah had never really been afraid of anything, but now he felt very afraid.

rocks

Just when Na-gah thought he could not go on, he saw light. *At last,* he thought, *I have reached the top!*

Na-gah walked toward the light. There was another crack in a rock. He squeezed through the crack. Na-gah was back outside of the mountain. He was at the *top* of the mountain! He was filled with joy! "I made it!" he shouted. "My father will be so proud of me!"

mountaintop

But his joy turned to sadness. He realized he could not go back down the mountain. Now he would have to live on top of the mountain forever.

Suddenly, Na-gah heard his father's voice. "Na-gah! Na-gah!" shouted Shinoh, as he walked across the sky. Shinoh looked everywhere, but he could not see his son.

"Father, look!" shouted Na-gah. "I am on top of the tallest mountain!"

---

realized: understood

   Shinoh was so proud of Na-gagh. Na-gah has climbed the tallest mountain! But Shinoh felt sad. *My son can never come down from the mountain,* thought Shinoh. *But because he was so brave, I will do something special. I will turn Na-gah into a star that will shine forever in the sky.* So Shinoh turned Na-gah into the North Star.

   That is why, the Paiute Indians believe, the North Star never moves. All other stars move across the sky, but the North Star stays in the same place every night. Only Na-gah, only the North Star, stays in one place, on top of the tallest mountain in the world.